Veins Of Emotions

RUPA BARDE

Kindle

She truly documents her journey over the last 2 years of her existence. She welcomes the reader into her life, documenting every experience, including her heartbreak, love, loss and happy times. Rupa's goal in writing the book is to share her journey, the obstacles she has overcome and her often not so straight road to recovery. Her message is simple, there are plenty of emotions we go through in our daily life which mostly teaches us many things, the good and the bad. It depends on us how we see that particular situation. Because all that matters is Perspective.

RUPA BARDE

Preface

Did you ever notice how a single drop of your blood passes by your veins all over your body to function. In the same way how your emotions pass through your actions.

That's why I had named as "Veins Of Emotions"

Veins of Emotions is a collection of micro poems by Rupa Barde.

It's a sweet gesture of my journey along with my feelings which I would love to share with all of you.

They've always said,

"This is nothing new, you will feel it in your breakup."

and I have always replied,

"With a smile, you won't understand"

Do you know why?

Because no matter what the world says, you should know what's going on inside you as you alone know what's the actual struggle you are battling.

Veins of Emotions

- RUPA BARDE

The unheard numbed emotions of an silence journey,
with a tale of pain, sadness, joy, love and healing.

Contents

Who was I in your Life?

You seem to be somebody else
But you showed something else
Your emotions were meaningful
But your words were a lie

Always fulfilled your desires
But I never thought about of mine
For you I was just a call away
But you never thought the same

It seems I was just your Google Map
Who always gave you right directions
Or maybe I was your fixed investment
Who always gave you interest
In the end,
all I was left as a giver.

Wings

Injured soul with a spark of appearance

Dig their own funeral in silence

But would always been there for others

Protected them like no one else did

Made them believe their scars are beautiful

Taught them to speak up for their rights

Leaded them to grow their wings

But never mentioned, about their own self.

Trust

Can anyone describe it in one word,
Loyal or Fraud?
Who really cares.

We live in a selfish world.
So what can we expect from others
As we within ourselves are a big liar.

So how can we expect from others?
As it's just a matter of fact.

Isn't it?

A eye contact would have been enough
Together holding our hands were like carrying a shelter
Walking besides were like carrying double baggage
Confronted rumours as in it's their jealousy and our purity.

Isn't it about us?
Or
Isn't the connection we had?

But we never knew,
Adjusting with groups would apart us
Misunderstanding would be it's reason
And Unplugging would be it's answer.

One Conversation

We looked at each other like we never want to look away

Together we were a package of mood buster

Like a free spirit still learning how to catch up their feelings

And the other side caution from being the wildflower

Intentions where always keeping it simple just like young and alive.

Treasuring unbelievable memories for better days

With time we build castle of happiness

Never imagined whether two unknowns could pair a circle

Felt like it's a fairytale story which became our reality

One Conversation,

Magically changed our entire perspective.

Upside Down

She blooms like a flower
He walks like a warrior
They visualise it differently
Before the season changes
They realise the need to wake up
From the imaginary world
That's all what the upper side says.

Made a move without sharing
Proved proofs instead of disappearing
Achieved success as a secret
And settled without announcement.
But did you ever listened,
What did you actually feel deep down?

Different

Two people,
Two lifestyles,
Two perspective.

One who is overthinker,
and the other one is an over analyzer.
One is full of positivity
and the other is full of confusions

They have different likings,
but tries sacrificing.
Two different hangouts zones,
but tries to mix up just for each other.
Love was pure,
but it's connection was weak
Misunderstanding was the disease,
and cure was it's separation

Only one thing remained the same,
both were 1st class Runner ups.

Shades

I know I'm still learning
To live my life again
I am still learning
As I know there will be a better days

I will never forget
People said I'm not good enough
People said I'm not worth it
People said I'm too young
What to do? When they say.

I have always told myself
One day I will change their mind
Because I will do everything I have dreamed of
And be my own shelter
Old mistakes that I have made
Won't repeat that circle again

As the old me showed me the things

Before I get to know the real me

I hope I'll never change

Even though when past reunite

I will keep those judgments as a silent secret.

Relive

Days are passing, better to be on track
Plenty of reasons I should never recall it.

But it's never the same when they ask me
Can't control my feelings, it's quite haunting.

It's been ages,
Tired of pretending and being lonely.

Don't you think I should have got an Oscar?
As no one caught me, not even you.

In Time

Long game filled with boundless memories
Pretending to be temporary fix
Conflicted by following rules
And tripping over it.

Should have told, how we felt way back.
As it's hard to bare, it ain't easy.
All I am waiting for a chance,
to make everything right.

Because these city lights,
feels like love nots ghost
and laughing behind our back.
Still there is time, let's run away.
Where it feels, home.

Excuses

From toxic surrounding

I could feel my heart speaking

They got the combination

And I wonder if you could lessen?

Appreciation

Do you give company for early mornings?
Like you did, for me.

Does lemon tea still reminds you,
How did it all start?
Does German language still reminds you,
Your confession for me?

First semester was full of roller coaster rides,
One month filled with abundance of memories
And blessings I would ever cherish for lifetime.

But I never knew miracles,
would take place so beautifully.
All I could recall,
You tried to explore as many you can,
but never tried to hide my originality.

If anyone teases you today by my name,
or if we meet by coincidence.

I hope you don't regret a single thing,
like I do.

Stranger

I am not Stranger to this gesture
Because of you I am quiddity
Even when they make an effort
I know I'll never feel the same

I have been down by the people
Too many emotions I had buried
Being cold-blooded nothing surprises me

I need a reason to feel,
and you gave me a season to feel.

On my mind phases running late nights
You are the Prosecco of my life
You have twisted my feelings
It's crazy how it all ended on these sheets

You came around like an firefly

Filled the light in my life

You showed me my ikigai

You knew I was a brontide

So you made me like a balter

So I could never numb for way too long.

It Matters

Sleeping is an advantage.
As it inhale all the secret conversations,
Which your presence couldn't.

It could grow your relation,
Or it might spoil your relationship.

Always remember,
Excuses plays its role,
And distance becomes it's key.

Before it's too Late

So many people, so many perspectives.
Nothing feels better than this.

Mind has become a prisoner.
Thinking about it, I meant it.
But do you mean it?

I am sorry for the way I am,
Got problems that I don't understand.
If I could go back in time,
I would never make it happen.

Will you slow down?
And let me explain.
Aren't you happy?
Everything is back and right.
Nobody can see it,

But I am better.

It's been since I have even breathed.

Yesterday I felt, I was just born.

So this is my time,

But I could hardly afford it.

You locked me up with your intentions,

While I was feeling low.

Don't you want to ask?

Will it have a happy ending.

I like me better, when it's You

Hello Sunshine,
I know we aren't,
where we said we will be,
when we just met.

I felt my heart for the first time,
Something burnt inside me.
As in my loneliness,
it just stopped.

You can't imagine,
I am stronger than the emotions,
which draws me down.
I don't want somebody like you,
I just want you,
And I only want us.

RUPA BARDE

But that's okay with me,

As I have been self musing.

So are you happy now?

It's You

Everything in your brain,

is telling you to walk away from me.

But everything else is,

looking for a reason not to.

I can see you're choking.

I just don't get it,

Why don't you say it?

If it's bothering you?

Disconnecting me,

won't help you out.

When you know,

we can confide in one.

Since you left me,

You are faking up captions,

Sarcastically socialising with others,

To make sure you are doing great.

But ask yourself,
is it giving you peace?

If you would have socialised with me,
Light would have guided you,
and you would have felt home.

Asterism

My days begins with your face,
Your smoky eyes say it all.

There's something in your head,
Not even curiosity can hold.
Unexpectedly we felt the same,
Never knew you could re-ignite me.

Then the twist played its role,
Rumours knocked my ear's,
and voices inside me can feel your lies.

You were my constellation,
But I was your consolation,
As we had asterism between us,
We lost our poudretteite.

Solivagant

When I was loving you,
you thought I was still trying.
Look today all I am standing alone,
with a broken heart.

All you did, spread lies.
They think it's my fault.
But now I see you as a thief,
one who took away my soul.

Today I am living,
for my responsibilities.
Disconnecting and hiding,
all alone.
Scheduled my routine,
for avoiding others.
And earning money,

for getting disappear.

Pretending to be normal,
but I guess I can't be the same.

Vividly

Vividly keeps going,
like a hallucination journey.
Doomed from within,
like a secret symphony.

I'm just getting by,
but this vividly,
filled with visions of collisions.

You were my prominent one,
my man of candour.

Together we were coasting.
Until you flinch, seeing your ex.
You had flicker your hidden vividly,
which broke me apart.

Time Travel

Can't stop the distance between us,
I wish it would be a dream.

Bits you will never confront,
stored confusion in your heart,
battling between your heart and head.

Working around like a robot,
Got alot on my mind back,
Though our love could be united.

But I'm here wondering,
are you brave enough,
to win back my love?
But I am,
not afraid to time travel.
All I'm afraid of is your lies.

Its Starts From You

Met you thousands of times,

but my journey never felt so peaceful.

I wish I could say you,

but I wasn't sure about it.

Nobody knew, not even me.

You would mean so much!

I used to meet you at midnight, in my dreams.

And the next day, I used to Roar.

You taught me,

not to be a people pleaser.

So I could live happily.

I wish dreams could become reality,

where I can feel each moment with you.

It's been ages now,

I am running out of time.

Can you check on me?

Its You & Its Me

Being loyal was your royalty,

Saying easy was your sarcasm,

Doing unsaying was your humbleness,

And being together was your pride.

There is nothing new,

you are on my mind.

But please, only be in there.

As I don't want you,

in front of me.

Because as a self gift,

This time I have found myself.

Scintilla

I still remember the lantern night,
those little ray of hope,
you were trying to give out there.

But you didn't realise,
Somebody's got an eye on you.
And that somebody was me!

Morning rays came in so soon.
As in just now,
we have started our conversations.

Your words and your laughter,
scintilla corners my heart.
Even your unsaid words,
drags me closer to you.

RUPA BARDE

I wish night would have lasted,

and we could stay,

a little longer.

Oblivescence

Did you ever tried to know,
What did they try to do?
They pulled me down by labelling .

I'm tumbling all way down,
but this time I ain't let it happen.
I will oblivescence you,
before they haunt me back.

I want to stream,
flashbacks like flashlights,
but my heart has frozen.
I wish it shouldn't be that tough,
because now it's my turn to fight.
Before I was sinking all day alone,
but now I'm fighting it.

Never knew this would become a race,

I need to run even farther.

As now it's time to breathe,

an Oblivescence breath.

Kontorōru

I gave you extra chances,
but now I am feeling,
I am losing myself.

Did you notice?
You dragged me down,
by holding your grudges.

I am scared,
to enter a room of manipulation.
All I was waiting,
for a miracle.

Then I met a stranger,
who treated me the way it must be.
Although you kontorōru me,
still I thought of you.

All I hope for one last time.

Could you ever treat me like he did?

Quagmire

I remember the long drives
Unstoppable talks, irreplaceable memories
Being wrapped with your love
And skipping negativity away

I knew things won't stay the same
But still I took a chance of faith
Maybe this time I won't be broken
But you proved me wrong

It's been too longs
I'm holding on the weight
I'm scared to move on
Feeling like I'm in a quagmire
But still my heart is struggling

Let's keep a silence for 5 mins,
Take a glass and toss,
for no more troubles.

Maybe be I'll see you next
But I would keep it straight
You were just a memory
Bright like a shining star
And lasted till bright light.

Hard To Decide

When things don't go your way,

all you could recall is me.

And me like always,

thought of helping you out.

But when I needed someone,

you never seem to be around.

And suddenly you are asking for it back?

Could you tell me where you have been?

Didn't even bother to see me once.

It took a while to understand,

All it was your selfish intentions.

Still I don't know what to say.

Don't you think,

Selfishness soaked our friendship?

And intentions buried the thought of it?

You were not the same like before
Or only I didn't understand?
I don't want to judge you so soon,
Still I want to hear it from you.

It's just even you are broken,
Which turned you on?
Or do you love playing around?

What's the actual truth?
Previous or Present?
Hard to decide.

You Are Dangerous

Look what you made me do
Look what you made me today
I'm not somebody, I'm not me.

I'm still breaking my heart
I can't get it out of my mind
Everytime I close my eyes
I am being haunted, I am bleeding.
You need to believe me!

I don't want to close my eyes
There's so many questions
I guess you don't know
what you have done.
Your words reminds me daily,
It's darkness within me.
Nobody does this to anyone,

Especially to their loved one's.

What have you done to me?

You made me so weak,

You are dangerous to me.

Goodbye

You disappeared just like a wind

Couldn't find the same vibe

You had walked away miles back

But your essence where all around

Every sip of green tea

Every bite of cheesecake

Every early morning walks

As if it's still the same

But this time I am all alone

Can't even imagine

How it all ended in one shot

Because goodbyes aren't what we decided

Separation nor do we wanted

Circumstances wasn't on our side

So we couldn't help it

All I know

Our togetherness was a dictionary

But we didn't know how come

Our dictionary had goodbye in it

Never got the chance to say goodbye

But if we could have got

It would have been much better than self musing

Silence

I use to sing along with the birds
Use to close my eyes to feel the wind
And capture every moment before it's late
In short, I used to be cheerful.

Didn't knew what was silence.
But today I guess,
I don't know how to be cheerful.
Silence has become my best friend
And maybe that's what you have gifted me.

But one day for a moment
I hold on hope
Just because somebody saw hope
Which turned me from being sober
Taught me by living together
Chased my dreams as it's theirs

... THEN ...

Silence just began a room of darkness

Which gladly lasts no longer

Until grace was poured.

Journey

Our story is yet incomplete
Maybe our paths would cross again

While walking at our favourite corner,
I could recall our flashbacks
Didn't regret nor do I blamed
Just wished our paths to reunite

Our Journey became like a journal
Don't know where it would end

Time became my best friend
Sticked so tightly, couldn't resist.
All I could admit,
In search of our paths,
I found me.

Acknowledgement

Thanks to every single person who encouraged me and supported me to write this book, my parents for always beliving in me and helping me chase my dreams.

I am also thankful to everyone who has ever walked out of my life, you are one of the reason how this book came today into existence.

Thanks to my fellow friends who helped indirectly with this book, I am eternally grateful to all of you.

Thank You.

Made in the USA
Columbia, SC
01 September 2022

66232988R00035